Wolfgang Amadeus MOZART

By Eric Tomb

Leopold Mozart was a very methodical man. When his eight-year-old daughter Nannerl showed a gift for music, he compiled a book of keyboard exercises for her to practice. The book contained minuets, marches, scherzos and other short pieces by several contemporary composers and Leopold was always careful to note down the date when Nannerl had mastered each one.

After a while, another name began to appear beneath the exercises. "Wolfgangerl learned this minuet in his fourth year," it might say or, more proudly, "Wolfgangerl learned this minuet and trio on January 26, one day before his fifth year, at half past nine in the evening, in half an hour." Years before there was any TV, or even electricity, you might have expected a four-year-old to be fast asleep at 9:30 on a cold winter night, but this one, this "Wolfgangerl," was wide awake at the piano with only a candle or two to light up his music.

Wolfgang was christened Joannes Chrysostomus Wolfgangus Theophilus Mozart* and he had been born in Salzburg, Austria on January 27, 1756. He and Nannerl (whose full name was Maria Anna Walburga Ignatia Mozart) were the only two of Leopold and Anna Maria Mozart's seven children to survive beyond infancy, but they were more than enough. Nannerl already promised to be an exceptional musician; Wolfgang was clearly a prodigy. In the days before both words got overused, they meant about the same thing as monster.

He was a fiery boy, excited by almost everything. Reading, drawing, arithmetic were to him just different kinds of play; when he was first learning arithmetic, he chalked numbers all over the walls, floors and furniture. Then he discovered music. A friend of Leopold's recalled that "As soon as he began to give himself to music, all his senses were as good as dead to other occupations and even his childish foolery and games with toys had to be accompanied by music if they were to interest him. When we . . . carried toys . . . from one room to another, whichever of us was empty-handed had to sing and fiddle a march."

After M. B. Ollivier's English Tea, Paris, 1766

*The first two names referred to the saint on whose day the boy was born; they were conventional and usually soon forgotten. The third, which was the name he actually used, was the name of his mother's father. The fourth, which came from his godfather, meant "beloved of God" in Greek; in German it was Gottlieb, in Latin, Amadeus. In his earlier letters, Mozart also used his confirmation-name, Sigismundus.

Leopold Mozart was just as strong-willed as his son, plus he was a lot bigger. He had made a respectable career for himself in the orchestra of the archbishop of Salzburg. He was also a competent composer and the author of one of the first textbooks on violin-playing. But he never rose above the rank of assistant *Kapellmeister* in the Archbishop's orchestra *(Kapellmeister* literally means "Chapelmaster," but it was the title used for the person in charge of any German musical organization). Sensing that Wolfgang had much greater prospects, he began to plan an ideal career for him. This started with a careful and systematic grounding in clavier (this was a general term for keyboard instruments, including both the harpsichord which was in common use at the start of Wolfgang's life and the piano which was just beginning to replace it), music theory and singing.

But Wolfgang never waited around for Leopold to teach him. He once asked to play the second violin part in a trio his father was trying out with some friends. Since he had had no violin instruction, Leopold reproached him for asking. "You don't need to have learned anything to play second violin," Wolfgang insisted and broke into tears when Leopold still refused. Finally allowed to play along "so softly that you aren't heard," he did so well that the regular second violinist soon stopped and let him continue alone. He went through six complete trios at sight and then tried the first violin parts. Those were a bit too hard for him.

It was also his own idea to start composing. He was only four when he showed his father his first clavier concerto. The manuscript was a mess of inkblots, but Leopold found as he read through it that it was clearly and correctly written, "but . . . useless because it is so . . . difficult that no one could play it." Yet that was just what Wolfgang had in mind: he expected that a concerto would take a lot of practice and seemed happy to find that he himself couldn't play what he had just written.

These displays of genius brought tears to Leopold's eyes — and practical schemes to his mind. In an age when most musicians were dependent on noble patrons — the members of the Salzburg orchestra wore court uniforms and dined with the servants — a few virtuosos and composers were beginning to make a living on their own. If Wolfgang and Nannerl could get to the larger cities of Europe, they had a chance for the fame and fortune that had always eluded their father. They would also benefit as musicians from experiences and contacts that were unavailable in Salzburg. Conveniently enough, Leopold also felt that it was his duty "to proclaim to the world a

Leopold Mozart after Jacob Fridrich

prodigy that God has allowed to be born in Salzburg . . . to convince the world of this miracle, especially in these times when . . . people deny all miracles." Just before Wolfgang's sixth birthday, he took his children on the road.

Although Salzburg was home to one of the best-run orchestras in the German world and could boast of musicians like Joseph Haydn's younger brother Michael, it was clearly toward the bottom of the European cultural ladder. In the tours he planned for his children, Leopold moved them up rung by rung, making connections with many of the interrelated noble families of Europe and letting their reputation spread before them. The first trip, which lasted only three weeks, took them to Munich, the nearest large city. It was apparently a success (no records remain) and eight months later he attemped a more ambitious tour. Stopping first at the small Austrian cities of Passau and Linz, Wolfgang and Nannerl created such a sensation that Leopold decided to move on to Vienna.

Capital of the Holy Roman Empire, Vienna was one of the most important and most musical cities in Europe. After a few performances at the houses (palaces, actually) of wealthy Viennese, the Mozart children were commanded to appear before the family of Empress Maria Theresa. A lot of their performance was really musical parlor tricks, like playing a clavier whose keyboard was covered by a cloth, which were impressive to nonmusicians but a matter of course to any professional, of whatever age. Wolfgang and Nannerl won the hearts of the courtiers as much by their behavior as their skill. When the Princess Marie Antoinette helped him up after he slipped on a highly polished floor, Wolfgang made a point of praising her kindness to the Empress. The court rewarded them with money and fancy dress clothes.

But there were already some signs that Wolfgang wasn't entirely suited to the rigors of a concert career. He was an affectionate and sensitive boy, who loved praise and attention but hated loud noise and confusion. The round of concerts in private houses — sometimes two three-hour-long ones in a day — that followed the success of the court performance soon led to his first serious illness. Leopold, who always looked at the practical side, guessed that the family lost a good deal of money during his two-week convalescence (they played for free, by invitation, in private homes, with the hope of money or a valuable gift if they pleased). But the setback seemed temporary and their success in Vienna was so encouraging that he bought a

After a portrait by Pompeo Batoni said to be of Mozart, 1770

carriage before they returned to Salzburg.

The roads were horrible almost all over Europe in those days and a good carriage was absolutely necessary if you wanted to travel any distance. Leopold clearly had a long trip in mind, but Wolfgang fell ill again and it was five months before the family set out. This time they passed slowly through southern Germany, where the towns were nicely spaced for a day's journey and the children gave their first public concerts, to the rich cities along the Rhine. By now Wolfgang was also performing on the violin and improvising on both harpsichord and organ. Sixty-seven years later, the poet Goethe still remembered the "little man with his wig and sword" he had once seen perform in Frankfurt-am-Main.

But Leopold was really aiming for the two great metropolises of northern Europe. Two months before Wolfgang's eighth birthday, the family finally arrived in Paris. Using Leopold's carefully assembled letters of introduction, they quickly made contact with local Germans. Melchior Grimm, a German whose writings were influential in France, wrote enthusiastically about Wolfgang and Nannerl; within a month the children were invited to perform at the court of King Louis XV at Versailles. The almost predictable round of public and private concerts followed. Delayed again by Wolfgang's illness, the Mozarts remained almost five months in Paris.

Then it was on to London. Here their success was at first even greater than in Vienna and Paris. Wolfgang and Nannerl were invited to play before King George III almost as soon as they arrived; a second royal concert followed some three weeks later. Their first public concerts were also spectacular successes. Then it was Leopold's turn to take ill. After his recovery, their momentum seems to have been broken. Although the Mozarts remained in England for fifteen months and performed at court a third time, the second part of their stay was barely satisfactory. The nobility, which was the backbone of the musical public, was out of town during the fall; by the next spring, they were occupied with the uniquely English oratorio season (featuring the classics of Handel) and had little time for foreign musicians. Leopold felt lucky to have broken even in England.

Wolfgang was a lot luckier. He was too young to worry about money so he had time to think about writing music. He had been composing for almost four years now and had published his first compositions in Paris. In his concerts he played his own compositions and sight-read and impro-

The Mozarts after Carmontelle, 1763/4

vised on the works of others. But the composers he met in Paris and London taught him new ways of looking at music. Johann Christian Bach, the youngest son of Johann Sebastian Bach and the current star of the English musical world, influenced Wolfgang's style more than anyone except his father. He was a much more imaginative and flexible composer than Leopold could ever let himself be and he and Wolfgang would sometimes improvise together at the clavier, the young boy sitting on the man's lap. Wolfgang's first three symphonies, written during Leopold's illness, when the household had to remain silent, show what he had begun to learn from Bach.

And it was in London, of all places, that he got his first big dose of Italian opera. Italians dominated European music at that time and opera was usually considered the pinnacle of Italian music. In France and Germany, native music-dramas still competed with Italian opera. In England, where music-making had recently given way to money-making, the Italians had the field to themselves (except during the oratorio season). All opera composers — even Germans living in England like Bach — wrote their music to Italian texts and Wolfgang met many of the leading Italian singers who were working in London. He learned to improvise Italian arias on given themes and determined to write an opera himself when he returned to Salzburg. Back in Paris, Melchior Grimm noted that he sang much more expressively than before going to England and predicted that he would have an opera performed in Italy before he was twelve.

The return trip to Salzburg lasted well over a year. There were so many towns in Holland, central France, Switzerland and southern Germany and Leopold decided that they all must want to see his children perform. Except for a near-fatal bout of typhus, which struck both Wolfgang and Nannerl in Holland, their journey was another monotonous string of triumphs. Wolfgang by now was a complete professional. He regularly stopped to try out famous organs in any city they passed through; he added conducting to the other features of his concerts; and he could write any kind of music he was asked to. In the Hague he produced a set of sonatas, some clavier variations, a concert aria and a short piece for piano and orchestra; in Paris a four-part *Kyrie* (the first section of a Catholic Mass, sung by four different voices); in Zurich a symphony and some nocturnes. When the family arrived in Salzburg shortly before his eleventh birthday, he was famous, well-paid and likely to become more so.

But he hadn't been to Italy. Northern Europe might be where the money was, but the best music still seemed to come from the South and a composer couldn't expect complete acceptance unless he had mastered the Italian style. After ten months in Salzburg, where Wolfgang caught up on his education and wrote some music for the archbishop's ceremonials, Leopold decided that he might be able to have an Italian opera produced in Vienna. The family rushed to the capital, only to have both Wolfgang and Nannerl take to their beds with smallpox. After a long recuperation, the children appeared again before Empress Maria Theresa; then Wolfgang set to work on his opera, *La finta semplice (The Pretended Simpleton).* Although the project was supposedly suggested by the Emperor himself, it kept running into intrigues and production difficulties; after four months work, the three-act opera, which contained twenty-six arias and an overture and filled 558 pages of music, was suddenly abandoned. Leopold complained to the court, but this may have aroused more hostility than sympathy: some people thought the Mozarts were getting a bit too pushy.

Wolfgang did manage to have a *Singspiel* (sung in German, with spoken dialogue, more like a musical comedy than an opera) called *Bastien and Bastienne* performed at a private house in Vienna and *La finta semplice* was produced when he returned to Salzburg. But although he composed more music than ever in the next eleven months in Salzburg, it was obvious that both he and Leopold were anxious to get on to Italy.

In 1769 Nannerl was eighteen and no longer a prodigy; Wolfgang's novelty was also beginning to fade. Toward the end of the year, when he had assembled enough letters of introduction, Leopold started south with Wolfgang. Their reception was the most enthusiastic yet. Northern Italy was at that time a jigsaw puzzle of small, semi-independent states, each with its own nobility, concert halls and musical societies. After public and private concerts, Wolfgang might be asked to show his tricks to the musicians and scholars of bodies like the *Accademia Filarmonica* in Verona, which appointed him honorary *maestro di cappella (Kapellmeister* in Italian), or the academies of Mantua or Bologna. In Bologna, the Mozarts also met the famous musical scholar Padre Giovanni Battista Martini, who fired Wolfgang's interest in the old-fashioned polyphonic style of composition. With Martini's help and encouragement, he composed an antiphon (a chart based on a religious text, the forerunner of the anthem) which won him member-

Mozart after Lorenzoni, 1763

After a miniature thought to be of Wolfgang and Nanneral Mozart, c. 1765

ship in the venerable Bologna academy, even though he was far younger than the required twenty.

An even greater honor met Wolfgang in Rome, where Pope Clement XIV awarded him the highest class of the Order of the Golden Spur. Few musicians — his contemporaries Karl Ditters von Dittersdorf and Christoph Willibald von Gluck among them — ever received any level of this order; the last one to earn the highest class had been Orlando di Lasso two centuries before.

But the greatest prize of the journey was the commission to compose an opera for the theater in Milan, which he received shortly after arriving in Italy. The opera, *Mitridate, rè di Ponto (Mithridates, King of Pontus),* was not to be performed until the end of 1770, so he had plenty of time to improve his Italian, study up on the tricks and conventions of opera and develop his skills as a composer. He had the chance to see the most recent operas and meet most of the leading Italian composers and singers — or at least the ones who weren't in Germany, France or England at the time.

He also had time for sightseeing, new friendships, joking around and growing up. It was at this time he started adding postscripts to Leopold's letters home; in a comical mixture of Italian and German, with occasional French or Latin phrases thrown in, he joked about the people and music he encountered. Music drew his sharpest attention. Shortly after their arrival in Rome, the Mozarts had heard a performance in the Sistine Chapel of the famous *Miserere* by the seventeenth century composer Allegri. This complex, nine-part work was considered private property of the chapel and no copies had ever been made. But Wolfgang wrote down the entire piece from memory after a single hearing and one of the chapel singers confirmed his accuracy.

After travelling as far south as Naples, where Wolfgang noted "Vesuvius is smoking strongly today," the Mozarts returned to Milan to work on the opera. He complained that he couldn't write much to his mother because his fingers hurt from writing so much recitative, but he finished the piece on time and it proved a great success. It was repeated twenty-two times (a very respectable number for the day) before they returned to Salzburg in the spring of 1771.

Fifteen-year-old Wolfgang was definitely too old for the prodigy business by now. It was time for him to look for a permanent job, preferably with an important court orchestra. A new commission offered the chance to both ingratiate himself with the Imperial Hapsburg family and return to Italy. In the late summer he and Leopold arrived in Milan to prepare a two-act opera, *Ascanio in Alba*, for the wedding of the governor of Lombardy, Maria Theresa's son Ferdinand. The work was another great success and the Mozarts stayed on in the hope that Ferdinand might have an opening for Wolfgang. But Maria Theresa, who may have been offended by Leopold's earlier complaints about *La finta semplice*, ordered her son not to "burden himself with persons who run about the world like beggars" and the job fell through.

They made it back to Italy one more time. Wolfgang had a commission for another opera, *Lucio Silla*, in Milan at the end of 1772. Although the piece was apparently successful and ran twenty-six times, it had unsettling, "romantic" elements that weren't to the Italian tastes; Wolfgang received no more opera commissions from Italy. Leopold's hopes of obtaining a post for Wolfgang from the Grand Duke of Tuscany in Florence were also dashed. The Grand Duke was another son of Maria Theresa and also had to follow her orders. For the first time in ten years, Leopold and Wolfgang prepared to settle down in Salzburg.

During their decade on the road, the Mozarts had received extraordinary consideration from the archbishop of Salzburg. He had granted Leopold leave after leave from his duties as court violinist and assistant *Kapellmeister* and had even appointed Wolfgang unpaid concertmaster just before their first trip to Italy. But Archbishop Schrattenbach died in late 1771. His successor, Count Hieronymous Colloredo, was a reformer and a disciplinarian, an "enlightened despot" who intended to rule his tiny realm according to the dictates of reason. This meant encouraging education and intellectual pursuits, but also abolishing popular holidays and running his orchestra on a very short rein. Since he knew he was right, he didn't care if he was loved. And he meant to be obeyed.

His reign actually began quite well for Wolfgang. He wrote a one-act opera in honor of his new ruler, surrounded it with a spate of symphonies, minuets, divertimenti (a divertimento is an informal sequence of short, sometimes dancelike movements), songs and sacred works. Archbishop Colloredo responded by assigning him a modest salary for his work as concertmaster. Aside from a short stay in Vienna during the summer of 1773 and a trip to Munich for the successful premiere of his opera *La finta giardiniera (The Pretend Gardener)* in early 1775, the Mozarts now remained in Salzburg for four and a half years. Wolfgang now had a chance to digest the musical impressions of the past ten years and solidify a style of his own. Although he was capable of very complex writing, he tended to refine and simplify the style that older composers like Joseph Haydn had created. The development and interaction of simple, memorable melodies and a delicate balance of instruments were his trademarks.

He produced a huge amount of work. In addition to an opera, *Il re pastore (The Shepherd King)*, which Archbishop Colloredo commissioned for the visit of the Hapsburg Archduke Maximilian, he provided chamber and church compositions for his master, a wide variety of pieces for private individuals and some that he must have created for his own pleasure. Although he developed differently in different genres, it seemed he couldn't help getting better in all of them. During this period he wrote his twenty-fifth symphony (in G minor, his first great symphony), his first piano concertos (some critics feel that *all* of his twenty-seven piano concertos are masterpieces) and all five of his violin concertos. By the time he turned twenty-one in 1777, he had a catalog of nearly 300 works.

But he was getting increasingly dissatisfied with Salzburg. After shining in the greatest courts and largest cities of Europe, he found life in a provincial archbishop's entourage boring and confining. He resented his status as a servant. And he found his employer more and more offensive. Archbishop Colloredo wanted to get his money's worth from his musicians. He wanted them to be on hand to perform quickly and efficiently whenever he required. He didn't want to share them with other patrons and seems to have resented Wolfgang's success in other countries. And he didn't like short people (Wolfgang was five feet four at the most). After Wolfgang had worked for him for several years, he declared that he knew nothing about music and should go study in Naples; then he condemned the Mozarts for "running around like beggars." (Where'd he get that line?)

In the fall of 1776, Wolfgang wrote Padre Martini in Bologna for advice. He hinted that he would like his help in returning to Italy, but all the old man could offer was praise for his work. The archbishop turned down Leopold's request that he and Wolfgang take leave for a concert tour. In the end, Wolfgang had to resign from the archbishop's services — or, more accurately and humiliatingly, he had to petition to be dismissed. On August 28, 1777, his petition was approved.

He left as soon as he could. Since Leopold's leave had been refused and Wolfgang seemed too trusting and easygoing to face the world on his own, his mother agreed to go along. They had no particular goal, only a general impulse toward the northwest with Paris or London as possible destinations. Wolfgang was really looking for a job — preferably as *Kapellmeister* — in a larger, more illustrious court or, failing that, to make some money and establish useful contacts by giving concerts along the way. Although he stayed behind in Salzburg, Leopold intended to supervise the entire operation by mail.

Munich was friendly, but there was no job there. Augsburg — Leopold's home town — had a pretty musical society and a very pretty cousin. Mannheim — Wolfgang got stuck in Mannheim. It was a small but distinguished city, the residence of the Elector Palatine of the Rhine (the nine German Electors sometimes ruled small states, but had amassed great wealth and power as the men who chose the Holy Roman Emperor). During the previous fifty years, the Palatine Electors had tried to make their capital a German Versailles, a palace city that was a center of art and culture. The current Elector, Karl Theodor, had especially concentrated on developing his orchestra, which became famous for its precision and expressiveness. Some, like Leopold Mozart, thought the Mannheim style too "mannered," but for many younger composers, the way the Mannheim conductors (themselves a new breed) used the well-disciplined orchestra to produce crescendos, long pauses and other dramatic effects was an inspiration to come up with new kinds of musical expression.

Soon after his arrival, Wolfgang was on good terms with the leading members of the Mannheim musical establishment and with Karl Theodor himself. But after a month of hopeful waiting, he found again that there was no job for him.

Since it was now the middle of winter, he proposed waiting in Mannheim until the weather was better for travelling. He insisted to Leopold that he wasn't wasting his time, but composing, teaching and making plans. These plans suddenly multiplied at the beginning of 1778, when he met the Webers, a family of travelling musicians. He was taken with the whole family, but especially with eighteen-year-old Aloysia, a gifted dramatic soprano. He made one short concert trip with Aloysia and her father, and then began imagining other possible destinations: Holland, Switzerland, maybe Italy.

Mozart after Helbling, 1765

These developments led to the first open conflict between Wolfgang and Leopold. Wolfgang's letters had been making light of his father's earnest advice ("I, Joannes Chrysostomus Amadeus Wolfgangus Sigismundus Mozart confess that the day before yesterday and yesterday (also often before) I didn't get home until midnight . . .") and Leopold decided that he lacked the will and discipline to make his own way in the world. Summarily ordering him to move on to Paris, he also decided that Anna Maria Mozart should accompany him, instead of returning to Salzburg as she had planned. Although the breach between father and son was soon smoothed over Wolfgang left Mannheim (and the Webers) very reluctantly.

Whatever fond memories he may have had from his visits fifteen years before, this time he found that he hated Paris. The weather was cold and the people were colder. Looking up old friends like Melchior Grimm and using his letters of introduction to the rich and powerful, he soon realized that he and they had little use for each other. When a friend offered him the post of organist at Versailles, an ideal stepping-stone to a high court appointment, he ignored Leopold's urgent admonitions and decided to turn it down. He and his mother had sold their carriage in Mannheim and he now found that without one the distance between appointments was immense and that no one really cared when he finally got there.

While Wolfgang was walking across Paris from possible patron to possible patron or student to student, Anna Maria sat patiently in the cold dark room they had rented. She spoke less French than her son, and at fifty-seven, was less inclined to push her way into unfamiliar society. After they had been in town for a month, they moved into a warmer, lighter apartment; but it was just then that Anna Maria took ill. Her symptoms were never clear and seemed at first to respond to the home remedies Leopold sent from Salzburg. She also agreed to have herself bled and, after that, her condition worsened rapidly. Fever led to delirium and coma and she died on July 3.

Wolfgang was devastated by his loss and had no idea how to explain to his father what had happened. He wrote Leopold about the performance of his latest symphony and mentioned that Anna Maria was still sick. Then he wrote a family friend in Salzburg and asked him to break the news. Although he seemed to take his wife's death calmly and replied with advice about Wolfgang's prospects in Paris, Mannheim and Salzburg, Leopold couldn't help implying that he had sacrificed his mother through his irresponsibility.

Within a few months, Wolfgang decided to return to Salzburg. He was beginning to make his way in Paris, but progress was excruciatingly slow. He had also quarrelled with Melchior Grimm, his chief patron in Paris. And he would naturally have to pass through Mannheim on his way home.

But Mannheim was deserted. The Elector of Bavaria had died and Karl Theodor, who hoped to succeed him, had taken his entire court to Munich; like many other itinerant musicians, the Webers had gone along. When Wolfgang himself reached Munich, he found that Aloysia and her father had both taken good jobs and that she was no longer interested in a composer whose career seemed to be going nowhere. When he wrote her an Italian aria as a declaration of love, she turned him down cold. He returned to Salzburg as slowly as possible.

Leopold had somehow patched things up with the archbishop and contrived to have Wolfgang appointed court organist. The pay was three times what he had earned as concertmaster and, even with the debts he had incurred on his trip to pay off, enough for a single man to live on. After the tribulations of the last year, he must have been relieved to settle down into a humdrum life at home. During 1779 and 1780, he composed steadily and brilliantly. Working with some of the new techniques he had picked up in Mannheim and Paris, he turned out three symphonies, two masses, a variety of concertos, divertimenti and smaller works.

But he had come to loathe Salzburg and the Salzburgers, who seemed to have no appreciation of music (especially his own). When he received a six-week leave to oversee the production of his new opera *Idomeneo* in Munich at the end of 1780, he stretched his absence to four months. There was lots of work to do, revising the opera to fit the talents of the singers on hand and going over every detail of the production (by mail) with Leopold, but Wolfgang had enough energy to knock out a five-act ballet, two arias, two songs, a wind quartet, a wind serenade and part of a Mass as well and then to join in the Munich Carnival festivities. Yet for once he responded immediately when Archbishop Colloredo finally recalled him to his service.

It may have helped that he didn't have to go back to Salzburg: the archbishop and his court were in Vienna to celebrate the accession of Maria Theresa's son, Emperor Joseph II. Then Wolfgang discovered that his master, who apparently greeted him quite cooly, intended to treat him more as a slave than a servant. He decided where Wolfgang would live and eat and forbade him to perform for anyone else. Coming from the great success of

Constanze Mozart after Hans Hansen, 1802

Idomeneo in Munich to the city where he had once been the darling of the nobility, Wolfgang felt cramped and insulted. Against Leopold's advice, he decided to resign. At first his letter of resignation was ignored; after a month, when it was obvious that he wouldn't reconsider, the archbishop's chamberlain hurried him out of his lodgings with a kick in the rear.

Wolfgang was too exhilarated to feel humiliated. He was free at last, in one of the greatest musical centers of Europe, and must have felt that anything was possible. The cultivated nobility were eager to have him perform in their houses and it seemed likely that he could make a living any way he wanted (he mentioned five choices to Leopold: getting a court job, teaching, writing operas, public concerts and publishing his work). He got the libretto of a German *Singspiel, Die Entführung aus dem Serail (The Abduction from the Seraglio)*, to work on almost immediately; in the year before the piece was finally produced, he made good progress in everything except getting a job. He also got married.

The Weber family had moved to Vienna, where Aloysia got a job at the German theater, in 1779. After the father died suddenly, mother Cäcilie had moved her family into a house where she rented rooms to make a living. Aloysia had married the actor Josef Lange (from whose painting of Mozart our front cover is taken), but there were still three young daughters on hand when Wolfgang moved into the house in the spring of 1781. Leopold was scandalized and Wolfgang agreed to find a new room four months later. But he had already been smitten by Aloysia's younger sister Constanze and he was soon trapped between Leopold, who tried (by letter) to break up the connection, and Constanze's guardian, who wanted to promote it. The guardian, who just happened to be a high official in the theater for which Wolfgang was writing his new opera, forced him to sign a contract promising to either marry Constanze or make her a cash payment. Constanze proved her love by tearing up the contract; Wolfgang proved his by marrying her anyway.

The marriage distressed Leopold, but so did everything Wolfgang did at this time. Ever since the trip to Paris, he sometimes seemed to think his son could do nothing right. In his letters from Salzburg, he harped on his impulsive, trusting nature and predicted that he would never make it in the hard-headed music world. "His main fault," he wrote, "is that he is much too patient or lazy, too relaxed, maybe at times too proud . . . qualities which make a person inactive. Or else he is too impatient, too eager and can't wait for anything. He is ruled by two opposite principles — it's all either too much or too little, with no middle way."

But at this time Wolfgang seemed to be following the middle way very well. *Die Entführung* was a notable success when it first appeared in July, 1782. Emperor Joseph II, an earnest but not very musical monarch, was both appreciative and a bit baffled. "Too beautiful for our ears," he consented, "but there are very many notes." "Just as many as necessary, your majesty," Mozart replied. The "extra" notes, which were simply Mozart's means of making the orchestral accompaniment more expressive than was then usual, made the opera famous throughout the German world. "The *Seraglio,*" Goethe remembered,"put everything, else in the shade."

Wolfgang and Constanze had planned to visit Leopold shortly after their marriage, but they were so busy setting up house, moving a few months later, preparing for the arrival of their first baby and trying to keep up with the hectic Viennese music scene that it was July, 1783, before they finally reached Salzburg. Their three-month visit, during which he met Constanze for the first time, must have reassured Leopold about his son's marriage, as his return visit to Vienna a year and a half later reassured him about his career. He attended the first of Wolfgang's 1785 concerts, where he played a new piano concerto for "a great crowd of persons of rank . . . The concert was incomparable, the orchestra excellent." The next day he heard three of the six string quartets Wolfgang was planning to dedicate to Franz Joseph Haydn. And he got to hear Haydn's unforced, unenvious opinion: "Before God and as honest man, I tell you that your son is the greatest composer I know, in person or by name. He has taste and, moreover, the greatest knowledge of composition."

Leopold himself had been the first great influence on Wolfgang's musical style, providing the basic rule and techniques of composition. Johann Christian Bach had shown him the way to greater warmth and inventiveness. Now Haydn, whom many others considered the greatest living composer, inspired both more careful organization and more expressiveness. But Wolfgang had already reached the point where outside influence enriched his style without changing it very much. In the next few years, it was actually Haydn who benefited by studying Mozart's sensitive instrumentation and his knack for simple, haunting melodies. Although Haydn was twenty-four years older, the two men admired each other unreservedly; their uncompetitive friendship may be unique in music history.

Mozart & Haydn (thought to be) after Rigaud

Wolfgang seemed to be prospering materially as well as musically. He earned almost as much in one concert as Leopold did in a year and he had students, opera contracts and publications to add to his income. Although he enjoyed an active social life, especially during the winter Carnival season, and even had a full-sized billiard table in his apartment, Leopold noted that "the household is extremely economical as far as eating and drinking are concerned." He returned well satisfied on April 23. It was the last time he ever saw his son.

Wolfgang's position was promising, but also precarious. With neither a regular job nor a patron to rely on, he was completely dependent on the favor of the public. As long as his concerts were popular and he could get commissions for new works, he would manage well. But if his popularity waned or his health failed, he had almost nothing to fall back on. Health was a particular concern. Wolfgang's constitution had always been frail; the rigors of his childhood travels and the serious illnesses he had undergone along the way may have weakened it further. In an age when sanitation, nutrition and disease were imperfectly understood, even a minor illness could prove fatal (four of Mozart's six children died in infancy). In the summer of 1784, he suffered the first of a series of troubling illnesses. He seemed well by September, but his current popularity led him to rush back to work and he never got enough rest for a complete recovery.

His major project after Leopold's return to Salzburg was another opera. Up to now, he had usually written music for old or mediocre librettos; he had frequently had to reshape the texts as well as provide the music. Now he teamed up for the first time with Lorenzo da Ponte, a fashionable Italian who had been appointed Imperial court theater poet in 1784. It was Mozart who suggested that they collaborate on the controversial French play *The Marriage of Figaro*, but it was the diplomatic da Ponte who made the cuts necessary to get the work past the censors and persuaded Emperor Joseph that Mozart was really good at opera.

Mozart was at the height of his concert career while he was working on *Figaro* and he had to turn out a steady stream of piano concertos, as well as smaller pieces for special occasions. For the visit of the Governor General of the Austrian Netherlands, he had to work up the music for a comedy *Der Schauspieldirektor (The Impresario)*. But *Figaro* made its way through all these interruptions, as well as the intrigues that such a controversial plot (it had to do with a servant teaching his master a lesson) called forth. Its premiere in May, 1786, was a magnificent success and it was repeated again and again until the late fall.

Soon afterwards Mozart left Vienna for the first time in over three years. The Hapsburg emperor was traditionally also King of Bohemia and the Bohemian capital Prague was the second city of the empire. *Die Entführung* had already created a sensation there; now *Figaro* was an even greater hit. When Wolfgang and Constanze visited one of his noble patrons in Prague at the start of 1787, the word soon got out that he was in town and he was persuaded to conduct a performance of *Figaro*, give a piano concert and present his latest symphony (number thirty-eight, now known as the "Prague Symphony"). At his concert, the largest crowd in memory called him back for encore after encore; around town he heard people singing and dancing to tunes from *Figaro*; he quickly signed a contract to produce a new opera for the fall season.

Da Ponte, who also had librettos for Mozart's rivals Martín y Soler and Salieri to work on, chose the popular story of the Spanish seducer Don Juan. While he was working on the text (which in Italian became *Don Giovanni),* Mozart, who had earned a lot of money in Prague, stopped giving concerts to concentrate on the music. But he continued to give lessons and may have given a few to the sixteen-year-old Ludwig van Beethoven, who was in Vienna for a few weeks. And he could never keep all his musical ideas to himself or to one medium: while working on his opera, he also turned out several arias and songs, three string quintets, *A Musical Joke*, the famous serenade *Eine Kleine Nachtmusik*, and a number of piano and violin pieces.

It was just at this time that Leopold Mozart's health began to fail. He was now sixty-seven and prone to a variety of ailments. In the middle of March, 1787, his condition rapidly worsened and Nannerl, who had married and moved away a few years before, rushed to his side. Hard work and then his own serious illness kept Wolfgang from joining them, but the prospect of death erased the differences that had arisen between father and son in the past decade. In early May, Leopold seemed to be improving, only to die suddenly on May 28.

It may have been this close contact with death that called forth much of the stormy, somber and sometimes terrifying music in *Don Giovanni.* Mozart's earlier operas had been mostly elegant settings of light-hearted comedies or classically restrained tragedies. *Don Giovanni* brought to the

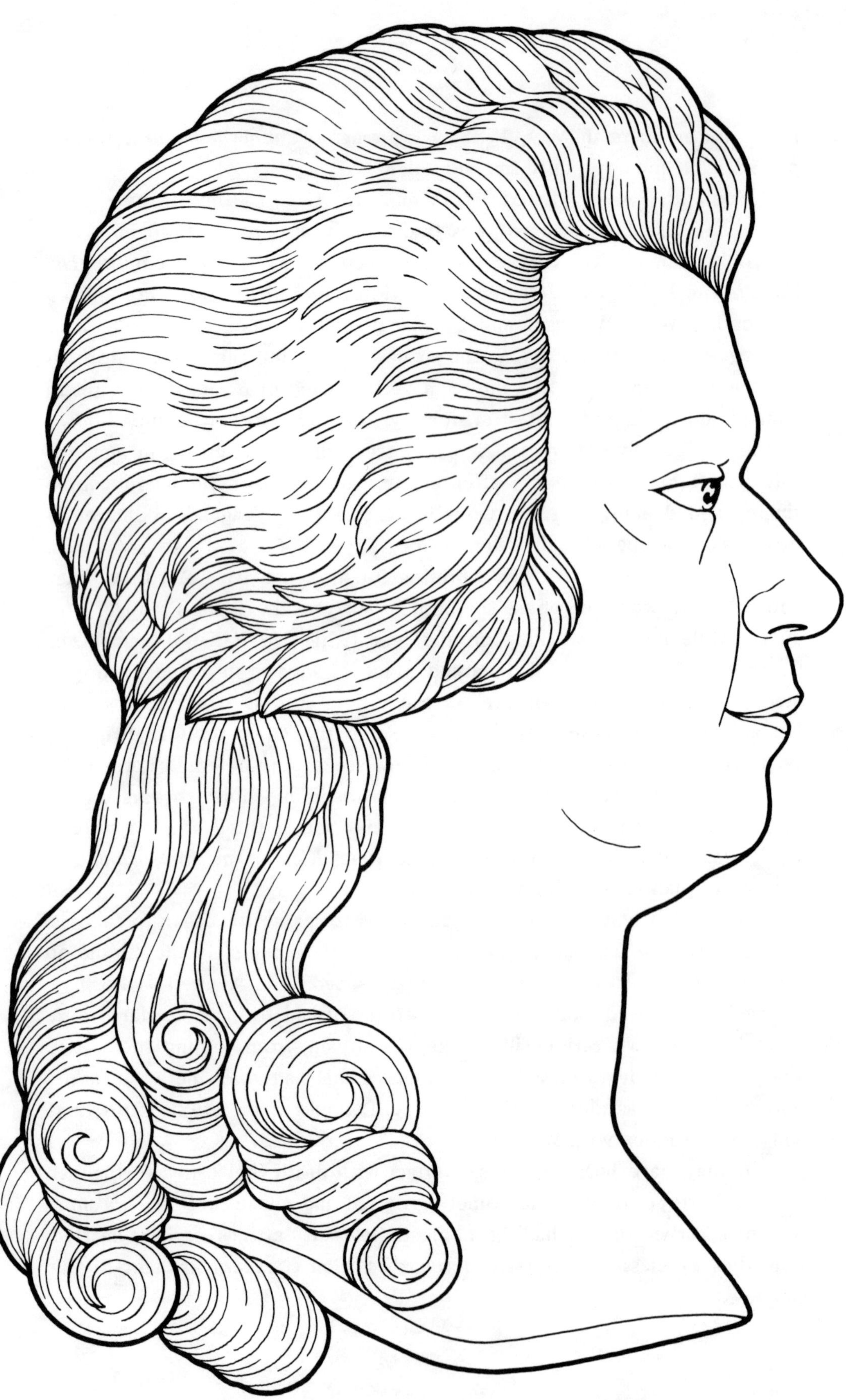

Mozart after a cameo by Leonhard Posch, 1788

stage a new kind of intensity, from its forceful overture (which legend has it Mozart composed the morning before the first performance) to the final scene in which the hero (or villain) is dragged down to hell by the statue of a man he had murdered. But the people of Prague seem to have expected innovations from Mozart and the premiere at the end of October, 1787, was another outstanding triumph. He was even thinking of staying on and writing more operas when he suddenly rushed back to Vienna.

An urgent message from da Ponte probably hastened his return. The famous composer Gluck was on his deathbed and Mozart hoped to succeed him as Imperial and Royal Court Composer. He did in fact receive the appointment, which carried with it a moderate salary and very light duties, in December. Now he finally had the regular income that should free him to compose as he wished. But he found that his other sources of money were drying up. Just when he was reaping such acclaim in Prague, he had been falling out of fashion in Vienna. *Don Giovanni* wasn't performed there until May, 1788, when it was only moderately successful. Da Ponte claimed to have asked the emperor his opinion of the work. "That opera is divine," he replied; "I would even say that it is more beautiful than *Figaro*. But such music isn't meat for the teeth of my Viennese." This may have given Mozart the chance to comment, "Give them time to chew on it!"Or it may not. Da Ponte had a good imagination.

The man whose opinion meant most to him was more positive. Haydn remarked that, "this opera isn't for the Viennese. It suits the people of Prague more, but it is mostly written for me and my friends." And again, "Mozart is the greatest composer now living in the world." But words wouldn't pay his debts and he was now acquiring more and more of these. He had probably reached the peak of his prosperity when Leopold visited Vienna in 1785, but he had never been very good at managing his finances and had begun borrowing from his friends even then. He could always expect to repay these loans after a successful concert or the premiere of an opera. Now that his Viennese audiences and music sales had dwindled and he had no contract for a new opera (he still had students), his borrowing became more desperate.

For a year, while *Don Giovanni* was being prepared and then performed in Vienna, Mozart turned inward. He wrote some songs and dances and his next-to-last piano concerto and arranged the instrumental scores of two Handel oratorios. In the summer of 1788, when he had no prospects that they would be performed, he wrote his three last, most personal and greatest symphonies. Although the three pieces are quite different, they all display a new depth of feeling. Leopold's death may have prompted some of the forceful outbursts in *Don Giovanni*; the three last symphonies may have in part reflected the loss of the most important person in Mozart's life.

In 1789, Mozart became more active again. Travelling with a noble friend, Prince Karl Lichnowsky, to Berlin, he also passed through Prague, Dresden and Leipzig. Although the journey made him only a small profit, it brought him back in touch with the larger musical world and showed him how high his reputation was outside Vienna. But when he returned home, he found that Constanze was seriously ill. The doctor's recommendation that she take cures at the spa in nearby Baden only added to his financial burdens; within five months of his return, he was borrowing money again.

The revival of *Figaro* that summer brought Mozart's name back before the Viennese public. He received commissions for improvements in other composers' operas and then for a new opera of his own. Working again with da Ponte, he produced a light, ironic comedy called *Così fan tutte (Women Are All The Same).* Its premiere in January, 1790, was a success — one newspaper commented, "To say that the music is by Mozart . . . is to say everything." — but there had been only six performances when Emperor Joseph died, and all theaters were closed for a period of national mourning.

The accession of a new emperor meant a turnover among court employees, including musicians. Like many who had been on the outside under Joseph II, Mozart hoped to find a well-paying post under his successor, Leopold II. But nothing came of his petition for appointment as *Kapellmeister* and music teacher to the royal family. Although Salieri and Count Rosenberg, two of his rivals in the musical establishments, lost their jobs under the new regime, so did his friend da Ponte. Mozart eventually received an appointment as deputy *Kapellmeister* at St. Stephen's Cathedral: this almost guaranteed that he would later become *Kapellmeister* himself, but for the time being, he received no pay.

In 1790, Mozart wrote very little music. Both he and Constanze were frequently sick and he had to depend on music lessons and borrowing to pay his bills. Toward the end of the year, he pawned his silver to buy a carriage and travel to Leopold II's coronation in Frankfurt-am-Main; with all the nobility of the Empire on hand, he hoped for a job or at least a com-

Mozart after a drawing by Doris Stock, 1789

Papageno after a design by Stürmer for The Magic Flute, 1816

mission. But he wasn't able to give a concert until after the coronation, when everyone else was leaving town. Brief stops in Mainz, Mannheim and Munich on the way home were more successful. As was often the case, travel seemed to have invigorated him and he was ready for work when he returned to Vienna.

All of a sudden, there was a great deal of work for him to do. Within two months, two impresarios offered him attractive contracts to compose operas in London. Haydn accepted a similar offer, but Mozart must have felt that his health was too shaky or that he had too many commitments at home. Taking leave of Haydn, he is said to have predicted, "I fear that this is the last time we will see one another." But he kept busily working on a variety of projects, from some pieces for mechanical organ (a commission he loathed), two string quintets and a number of songs and dances, to his last piano concerto and a *Singspiel, Die Zauberflöte, (The Magic Flute).*

This was a grand allegorical fantasy, written by his actor friend Emanuel Schickaneder, which contained many disguised references to the rituals and doctrines of Freemasonry. Mozart had been a Mason since 1784 and had seen both Haydn and his father join lodges. For him the Masonic movement provided not only a realization of eighteenth-century ideals like reason and brotherhood, but also a close circle of friends. It was his lodge brothers who lent him money during his most trying times; he may have felt that *The Magic Flute*, with its story of trials and initiations and its glorification of married love, was a reflection of his own experience.

While working on his *Singspiel*, Mozart received another, very mysterious commission. A tall, gaunt, cadaverous stranger asked him to secretly compose a funeral mass. It later turned out that the stranger was an agent for a musical nobleman who wanted to perform a Requiem for his recently deceased wife and pass it off as his own. But Mozart never knew this; with his own health rapidly declining, he was tempted to feel that he was writing a Requiem for himself. At the same time that he was trying to infuse *The Magic Flute* with the noble philosophical ideals of the Enlightenment, he expressed his deepest religious feelings in the Requiem. In a letter to da Ponte, he called it his "swan song" and vowed to finish it.

But he never did. Another urgent commission, to produce an opera, *La clemenza di Tito (The Clemency of Titus)*, for Leopold II's coronation as King of Bohemia, arrived in July, 1791. With less than two months before the coronation, he had to drop all other projects. Though the Prague premier was only moderately successful, it earned Mozart twice his usual fee for an opera and seemed to re-establish his position in the emperor's musical establishment. In spite of his ill health, he rushed back to Vienna for the September 30 premiere of *The Magic Flute*. This was a more marked success; with his finances temporarily in order, he went back to work on the Requiem and also turned out the beautiful Clarinet Concerto and a Masonic Cantata.

He broke down in November. Sensing that he was dying (he even thought he might have been poisoned), he found that he could make no progress on the Requiem. Constanze took the score away from him and forced him to rest, but he tried to go back to work as soon as he felt better. In a few more days he was bedridden; his hands and legs began to swell and he suffered fits of vomiting. In early December, he recovered enough to sing parts of the Requiem with some friends, but he was now talking of imminent death and telling Constanze how to arrange his affairs. He lost consciousness late in the evening and died shortly after midnight on December 5, 1791. To Constanze's sister Sophie, who had helped tend him in his final hours, his convulsive breathing seemed to echo the kettle-drums in the Requiem.

It was once commonly believed that Mozart died impoverished and forgotten and was buried in a pauper's grave. But casual burial was not unusual at the end of the eighteenth century and Mozart's career was actually on the rise during his last year. If he had lived, he might easily have enjoyed the spectacular success that had met Haydn in England; he might finally have received a well-paying position in Vienna or some other German city; he might even have become (instead of Haydn) the teacher of Beethoven, who was about to move to Vienna largely because it was Mozart's home.

Even without these "might haves," he was already recognized as one of the greatest composers of his time (only Haydn had a higher reputation). Although his admirers sometimes complained that his music was too complicated or too emotional, in a few years, the same music seemed serene and restrained next to the new compositions of Beethoven and audiences began to marvel at the amount and quality of work Mozart had poured out in the thirty-five years of his life. But he had spent thirty-one of those years composing; music was for him not just a way of making a living (or he might have made a better living), but his whole life.